PORSCHE

PORSCHE

Chris Harvey

Contents

INTRODUCTION

Generations come and generations go, but Porsche sporting cars seem to go on forever. Their timeless appeal can only be seen as a tribute to the genius who inspired them, Professor Ferdinand Porsche.

Early days

Previously, Professor Porsche had designed all manner of machines, culminating in the first Volkswagen people's car in 1936. By the 1930s, Professor Porsche was running his own design studio, producing blueprints for everything from racing cars to tanks.

Germany was his adopted home, and there Hitler was persuaded to let his studio produce a glamorous com[...] tion version of the austere Volkswagen for the Berlin-[...] Rome Axis race in 1939. The race never happened, b[...] two of the team cars survived as an inspiration for the [...] Porsche family to set up a new manufacturing compa[...] Gmund, in their native Austria, after the war. Times w[...] hard and they made their first cars from spare parts, [...] from old Volkswagens.

The first car to bear the name Porsche was design[...] the professor's son, Dr Ferdinand Porsche, along line[...] out by his father, who was by then more than 70. Its [...] Volkswagen engine was reversed to lie ahead of the [...]

s and carried in a tubular frame, a layout that can still
en today in racing Porsches. Their second car, with a
r Volkswagen Beetle-like body, had the engine in the
r place behind the rear wheels to make more room
ring – a configuration that survives today in the
c Porsche 911 series.

Spyders are coming

hese first cars in 1947, hundreds of combinations
een tried on similar themes.
old Professor lived long enough to see high-
mance versions of the touring cars win their class in
e Mans 24-hour race in 1951 as they established
elves in rallying at the same time. The publicity
d sell the production cars, and never since then have
he been out of competition. Ultra-light versions of the

mid-engined design had skimpy open bodies and adopted
the Italian name Spyder, which had originated on
horse-drawn racing carriages that darted along like
insects. Competition coupés with the same high-revving

The earliest 1100 cc coupés (below right)
*with their rear-mounted engine and
Volkswagen-style platform chassis, could
easily be distinguished by a money-saving
split windscreen; the same basic lay-out has
been carried through to today's* 911SC *(left),
but with no money spared on refinement.
The latest racing cars* (bottom right), *such as
the 956 seen in the pits in 1984, were every
bit as refined, but stuck to the mid-engined
format established by the very first Porsche.*

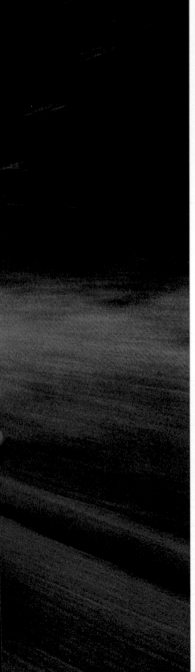

engines were soon called Carreras after early success in the Carrera Panamericana road race in Mexico. Such victories helped establish an even bigger market for Porsche on the US West Coast than in Europe.

The Spyders were developed to such an extent that they could go grand prix racing in open-wheeled form in the early 1960s. New engines were built as a result with even more power, and open sports cars dominated the last of the great road races, the Targa Florio in Sicily. At the same time, the basic production cars were becoming faster and more luxurious to meet market demand. Work on the 911 series started as early as 1956, with the first version seen in 1963.

The sports racing cars became ever faster, until the awesome 917 hit 240 mph at Le Mans and needed dr of the highest caliber to control it. Eventually these incredible cars became more manageable even whe they were turbocharged to stay ahead of the oppositi Such work soon found its way into the 911 series for t Porsche Turbo, which won the world's fastest car title Britain in 1984. Open versions of the 911 took the nam Targa, and ultimately Spyder.

Like dinosaurs, the 917s had to die, but their spirit survived in scaled-down versions that took a string of at Le Mans, evolving into today's all-conquering 956 a 962 endurance racers.

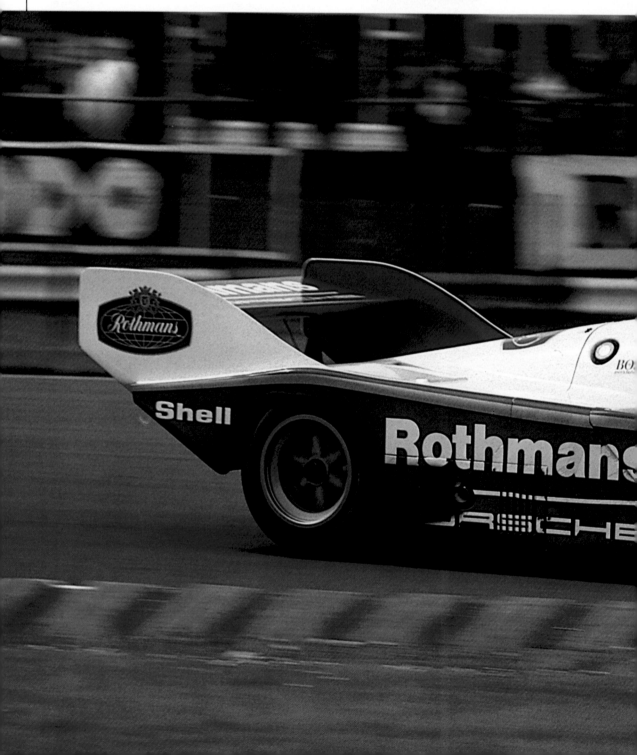

technology

middle of the 1970s Porsche were strong enough to
e the world oil crisis that spelled financial doom to
makers of luxury goods. But not before they had
back to their roots to produce another Volkswagen-
cheap sports car, the 914. This philosophy was
over into today's 924 series of front-engined
hes, with the complementary 928 and 944 luxury
coupés.

sche have never stopped designing things. Their
has been responsible for all manner of high-tech-
products, plus a formula one engine

that currently powers the highly successful McLaren grand
prix cars. Truly, Porsche have become the sporting car
maker for all seasons, with still the same family in control,
headed by Dr Ferdinand Porsche.

*The 956 has been all-conquering in world
endurance championship racing,
particularly in the hands of Belgian Jacky
Ickx, usually partnered by Germany's
Jochen Mass, or the Briton Derek Bell. Ickx
and Mass's works 956 is pictured here at
Silverstone, UK, in 1983.*

THE FAMOUS BEETLE MARCHES ON

The first Porsches were kept as simple as possible to make production easier, a fact highlighted by the designation, 356, their original planning code. These models might have had no name at first, but they soon established a character for Porsche that has not deserted the marque: they were of superb quality despite the early piecemeal methods of production. They were also fast because they had highly streamlined bodies and held the road well if the driver was good enough to cope with so much of the weight at the back. If the driver was not so good, the car handled like a pendulum, with the tail swinging from side to side. This strange ability, or lac meant that you either loved the car for the nimble way could be induced to negotiate tight corners, or hated because you couldn't control it – factors that have sta with the rear-engined variants of the marque to this d

of the reasons for putting the engine so far back,
from leaving more space in the passenger
artment, was that it gave the Porsches superb
n on rough roads, of which there were many in
e just after the war. Porsches still show an amazing
to climb hills.

earliest 356s were almost invariably fixed-head
s because they were meant for quiet, well-insulated
g, although a few more expensive but very civilized
rtibles were made along similar lines.
as natural that Porsche should retain close links
olkswagen because they still held patents on many
German car's features. All the early 356s used
wagen running gear, modified for better perform-
It was partly for this reason that they proved to be
eliable, another factor that has contributed so much
marque's enviable reputation.
1950 demand was high enough for Porsche to start a

move back to their old headquarters in Stuttgart. The move
was not an easy one; the works were occupied by the US
forces' motor pool. However, already the Volkswagen was
selling well in America and it was not difficult for an
Austrian-born car importer, Max Hoffman, to start selling
them as a sporting version of the Beetle. By 1954 he was
taking a third of Porsche's production, and later American
sales reached 70 per cent.

Throughout these early years, the Porsche engineers
behaved like all Porsche engineers have done since – they

*The distinctive style of the bubble-topped
Volkswagen Berlin-to-Rome racer (below
right) formed the basis for the 356 body,
which was subsequently marketed as the
Speedster with no top at all. These
Beetle-like open cars (left and bottom right)
have now become a prized item in any US
collection.*

could not resist making improvements to their cars, no matter how painstaking. In major ways, the engine was enlarged from 1100 cc to 1500 cc in easy steps, and a special version for competition offered as an option. Windscreens became one-piece as soon as the tools to make them could be bought, and even the old throttle-cable was replaced with a more reliable rod.

In 1954 Porsche began making special models for America, with one of the most emotive being the chop-topped Speedster, a lightweight sports car that appealed to fresh-air fanatics.

These cars were also attractive to a vocal minority because they were so light, but there was not much profit margin because they had no luxury fittings. Porsche were quick to identify this problem and saw a better future in more luxurious sports cars. They had no intention of expanding into mass-production where they would have had to compete with established giants. So that was the end of the Speedster.

The new philosophy

The models that followed, the 356A, 356B and the 356C, were the results of constant development on the original theme. But there came a point where no more power could be extracted from a normal engine to give either more performance or the same when the weight of even more luxurious fittings had to be hauled along. It was also apparent that the 356 had to be made bigger to cope with a population of ever-increasing physique.

Work had been going on for years on the car to replace the 356, the 911, which eventually went into production in 1964. The last of the 356s continued to be produced alongside it until orders for the new model built up to such a degree that Porsche could concentrate on the 911. But that last 356, the Carrera 2, was a wonderful car descended straight from the racers that dominate the next chapter.

The light weight of the Speedster (below) *soon made it an attractive proposition for competition along with the Carrera versions of the standard coupé. The fastest of the 356s was the last, the Carrera 2* (right and over page), *with a full two-liter four-cam racing engine. It was gradually modified until it reached C-specification in the 1964 model.*

To the purist's eye, the type 356A, pictured in silver Super 75 1 600 cc form (below and left inset), presented one of the cleanest and least-cluttered early Porsche forms . . with the Carrera 2 (right inset) presenting an emotive ending to the early part of the Porsche story.

THE ORIGINAL RACERS

From the start, all Porsches were designed to be able to acquit themselves well in competition, even if that was not their primary purpose. But some *were* designed purely for racing or rallying, with any form of touring ability as an incidental bonus. These cars had a dual function in that they provided not only publicity for the marque, but a constant feedback of information on how new ideas fared in the most extreme circumstances. The usual progression of development on these mobile test beds was more power, followed by better handling to cope with it.

The Berlin-to-Rome Axis prototype never made a race, but the first open car that bore the name Porsche did. It was sold to a Swiss customer called Kaes, who promptly won his class in a race at Innsbruck in 1948.

After that a succession of customers, often wealthy Austrian or German noblemen, took the early Gmund alloy-bodied coupés to victory in racing and rallying, notably Prince Joachim zu Furstenberg in the Swedish Midnight Sun Rally in 1950 and later Baron Fritz Huschke von Hanstein in all manner of events. But it was not until Le Mans in 1951 that the factory could afford to compete officially and then they immediately won their class with a coupé!

German Volkswagen dealer Walter Glockler had cut the top off one of the Gmund coupés, reducing the weight even further for short-distance events in which aerodynamics

The Spyders (below) featured a tubular chassis called a space frame – because, when viewed as a whole, there is more space between the tubes than area of metal – like that on the first Porsche, with, initially, a skimpy open body and later, by 1964, when Jo Bonnier was pictured (right) competing in the Targa Florio, a much-modified version featuring a rear spoiler.

were of lesser importance, and subsequently sold it to Hoffman, eventually giving rise to the Speedster cult. Glockler was then to enjoy a great deal of support from the works with a series of specials based on frames like that used by the first Porsche. These frames were lighter and stronger than the normal platform chassis, but cost a lot more to make, so they did not find their way into production cars. But just about everything else on these 'spyders' did. The engine capacity was increased to 1500 cc, and these units doubled up for the coupés – which kept the normal chassis.

The Spyders were then developed by the factory into the legendary Type 550, which was capable of 140 mph.

A new engine

Coupés were most frequently used for tiring races like the Carrera Panamericana, but it was to be a 550 that won its class in this event in 1953. By that time the 1500 cc

pushrod engine was at the peak of its development, Porsche produced another power unit, with four over cams and far more potential. The Spyder then beca known as the 550/1500RS, for *Rennsport,* or circuit racing. Notable victories included class wins in the c Italian road race, the Mille Miglia, in 1954 and at Le N

Technical development ran riot and Porsche Spyc soon received five-speed gearboxes, which subseq found their way into road cars, and even four-cam er for coupés called Carreras. By 1956 the number of modifications to Spyders were reflected in their designation, Type 550A/1500RS, which was freque down to RS. Their name might have been long-wind they won races such as the 1956 Targa Florio for Un Maglioli.

Continuous development led to a version called th RSK in 1957, the K describing the shape of its new fr suspension; the swing-axle rear suspension was als

ed with a more sophisticated coil spring system, and
rks cars became fast enough to challenge for the
lead in top races like Le Mans.

rand prix route

hey were stripped down, the sports cars also
competitive in the new formula two, normally
ed for open-wheeled racing cars. Carreras won the
Rome-Liege rally in 1957 and 1959; more highly
ped versions of the RSK, called RS60s, won sports
nts in 1960; and open-wheeled variants took first
cond place in the German Grand Prix for Jo Bonnier
olfgang Count Berghe von Trips.
che were suitably encouraged to build a formula
r, powered at first by the four-cylinder, four-cam
– with which American hero Dan Gurney took third
n the 1961 world championship – and eventually
eight-cylinder engine for 1962. This proved too

expensive, and Porsche quit formula one, although
lightweight Carreras with Italian Zagato bodies raced on
with great success until at least 1964.

In sports racing and hill-climbing, the RS60's successor,
the RS61, became the W-RS with a blend of Zagato nose
and Spyder rear bodywork. These cars were later known
as Type 718s after their engine serial and eventually their
two-liter four-cammer found its way into the 356 Carrera to
produce the formidable Carrera 2.

*The Porsche Spyder's timeless shape
disguises its age, which is revealed to the
keen eye by such period features as steel
wheels in place of the alloy ones that have
become a standard fitting on modern
machinery.*

Corrado Cupellini is pictured here racing his Porsche Spyder, the designation RS60 indicating that it was built in 1960.

The first Porsche (top left), with its primitive split windscreen, was a Spyder, the shape changing very little by the time racing machines had reached the 550RS design with their distinctive rear engine ventilation grilles (bottom left). The first major change to the competition Porsche's appearance was when they went open-wheeled for grand prix racing. Jo Bonnier is seen here (right) competing in the British grand prix at Aintree in 1962 with his car featuring the prototype eight-cylinder engine (inset) – surmounted by the typical Porsche cooling fan – that formed the basis of the production 911 power unit.

Porsches became popular in all forms of competition as was demonstrated by this Carrera in the 1964 Monte Carlo Rally (far-left). The formula two car (above), and the RS61 Spyder, pictured racing in 1975 (left), shared the same four-cam engine in differing states of tune.

THE CAR FOR ALL SEASONS

The 911 has to be seen as the car that even Porsche could not kill. It was a long time, seven years, in the making, and since then gives every indication of being immortal. In 1972 it seemed to have reached a peak that could not be surpassed with the fabulous Carrera RS, introduced nine years after the first model was shown. There were factions at Porsche who were convinced that it would have to be replaced by a newer car, one of their projected front-engined series. But such was the continuing demand for 911s that the later cars have never been able to oust it in the sales race. In the 1980s the 911, in turbocharged and normally aspirated forms, has found a new lease of life. It is be produced in fully open form and soon with the most advanced forms of four-wheel-drive, to keep it at the as an all-time classic.

Like the 356, the 911 was effectively designed by Ferdinand Porsche. When pressed by advisers to m a much bigger car than the 356, one that might comp with the likes of Mercedes in the saloon car field, he

ced a saying straight out of Austrian folklore:
·maker, stick to your last.' He meant that Porsche had
·successful by confining their manufacturing efforts to
s cars that were like no others.

greatest Porsche?

established family tradition Dr Ferdinand's son, also
Ferdinand, designed a timeless body only slightly
than that of the 356 outwardly, but a lot roomier
. It had a front luggage compartment that was big
jh to take a set of golf clubs and very wide doors,
pleased the Americans. But like the 356, it was built
latform chassis with an air-cooled engine mounted
rear. Dr Porsche did not want to change his basic
ct that much.
as introduced as the 901, although that designation
oon changed to 911 to avoid conflict with Peugeot,
e models had long had a zero in the middle of their
s. And it continued with every conceivable variation
on its new flat six-cylinder engine, based on that
used in the earlier grand prix cars. At first, a
capacity of two liters

was enough, with a high-performance version, the 911 S, as
an option. Soon after production cars were built with Targa
tops, which had a distinctive built-in polished alloy roll cage
aimed at meeting anticipated American legislation against
the completely open car. These 911s, in fixed-head and
Targa forms, had ever-increasing engine capacities,
through 2.2 liters to 2.4 and ultimately 2.7 for lightweight
versions called the Carrera RS. They were built to qualify
Porsches for production car racing and became wildly
popular as road cars, much to Porsche's surprise.

To many enthusiasts, the 2.7 Carrera RS is still the
ultimate Porsche with its combination of superb
performance – up to 150 mph – and lithe handling as a
result of its low weight. After that, the 911s became heavier,
partly because American safety laws meant that they had

*The early 911s – below is a 1967 S model
with its special 'five-star' alloy wheels – were
light and lithe machines running on relatively
narrow tires.*

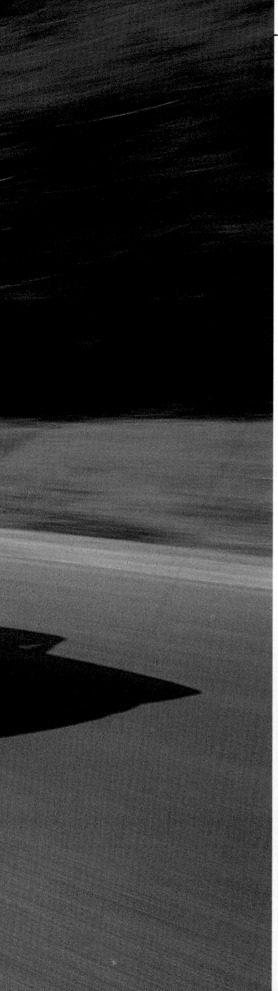

to have substantial bumpers. But it was partly because there was still more money to be made from very luxurious cars, and by 1975 the fastest 911 was a turbocharged version called the 930.

Ultimate development

These cars were called 930 because they looked quite different from a normal 911, with their very wide wheels and arches in bodywork taken from a road-racing 911 called the Carrera RSR. Everybody knew the 930 was a 911 at heart, and people got over the conflict by calling it simply a Porsche Turbo. It was such a fast and exotic car, however, that it seemed as though it must be the 911's swansong. Surely not even Porsche could develop it further?

But develop it they did, and in 1982 the first fully open 911, the Spyder, was introduced alongside the Targa and fixed-head coupé, now that the threat of American safety legislation had receded. The advent of highly developed four-wheel-drive cars, such as the Audi Quattro, which offers surefooted performance in the most adverse conditions, has resulted in Porsche following that path with the 911, too.

The light weight and superb flexibility of the Carrera RS (left) built in 1972 and 1973 – and almost invariably painted white with blue lettering – has made it one of the most desirable Porsches, even while the 911 continues in production with an engine enlarged to 3.2 liters in its latest, normally-aspirated, form. From 1974, larger bumpers had to be fitted – as on the red coupé (below) – to meet US safety regulations, which meant that all 911s which followed were inevitably heavier.

The close affinity between competition Porsches and their road-going relatives was never better demonstrated than when the bodyshell of the 1974 Carrera RSR and much of its running gear was used as the basis of the Turbo road car in 1975. Subsequently this classic wide-wheeled shape has remained substantially unaltered in the latest Turbos

One of the delightful aspects of the Porsche 911 and all its variants is the functional nature of every fitting. The bumpers of the blue 1978 911SC (left) retract on hydraulic rams under minor impact, while the driver's mirror of the 1980 SC in white 'Martini' livery (top) is electrically adjustable from the cockpit; and all current Porsche 911s have the very effective headlamp washers pictured on the 1975 Turbo (above).

BELL and CO. 1
Business Secretarial Services

John Bell

8

al Tyres Tonbridge

The Turbo was built initially to qualify a derivant of the 911, the 934, in grand touring races. This form of competition was governed by rules which stipulated a minimum weight – with the result that the 934 competed virtually unaltered from road form, making it one of the most luxurious racing cars ever built!

The definitive shape of the 911 has
remained unchanged since 1963 with only
minor modifications, such as the optional
'picnic table' rear spoiler to improve
stability at high speeds (left inset) and the
Targa top as fitted to the example from
Germany (right inset), which also featured
935-style front wings.

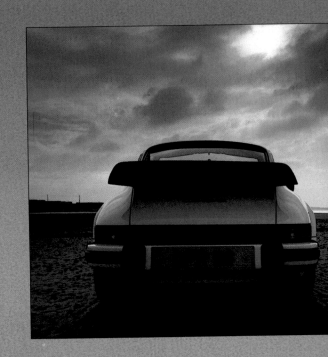

Aerodynamics play a vital part in the performance of a car like the Turbo, capable of more than 160 mph. Despite the confusing mass of regulations imposed by countries throughout the world, Porsche have managed to keep the frontal aspect of the car (left) as clean as possible, although they have had to fit the large spoiler at the back (above) as standard on the Turbo because of its high performance.

The Turbo-style front air dam with its brake cooling ducts can be seen clearly on the red 911 competing in a classic hill climb (left), while the yellow 2.4-liter Targa (top) has been fitted with a later type Turbo rear spoiler. The graphics of the rear logo are typical of the early 1970s and had given way to a far less pronounced script on the red Turbo (above) by the time it took the World's Fastest Car title in Britain in 1984.

THE FABULOUS RACING PORSCHES

Before 1964, Porsche were very much the underdogs in international sports car racing. They fielded relatively small cars that, although they almost invariably won their classes, were rarely in contention for outright victory. The Targa Florio was a notable exception, being run on such a tortuous course that the larger, heavier, sports racing cars were left behind by the smaller, nimbler Porsches. The long mountain climbs that were popular in Europe also developed into a battleground between Porsche and Ferrari (with their Dinos) because this form of competitio was limited to a two-liter capacity. In addition, Porsche d well in races for grand touring cars because their standa product was highly competitive when it did not have to fa purpose-built racers.

was in this area that Porsche started to reach for the
with the 904 in 1964. It was an exceptionally pretty
l-engined machine styled by the third Ferdinand
sche that astounded everybody by taking second place
e Monte Carlo Rally in 1965 – on snow-covered roads
t were a complete contrast to the normal sun-kissed
nac found in the GT events. The 904's technology was
ied over into the 906 in 1966 with the engine capacity
starting to rise, from 2 liters to 2.2; a lighter Type 910
built along the same lines to win the European
untain Championship. As a further development of the
the Type 907 – Porsche designations can be very
using – was able to run as high as fifth overall at Le
s, alongside ultra-lightweight 911s called the 911R.
ter that, variants of the 911S had three golden years in
rnational rallying as the 907 turned into the 908 with a
e-liter, eight-cylinder engine. These early 908s came
in an ace of winning the world sports car champion-

ship, with an even lighter Type 909 Bergspyder (mountain
spyder) supreme in the hills.

Taming the monster

From the 908 and 909 sprang the 908/2, followed by the
908/3, one of the most successful Porsche sports racing
cars ever built. These three-liter prototypes were so
successful that international racing regulations were
rewritten to allow series production cars to compete on
equal terms with engines up to five liters. Porsche replied in
1969 by building enough of their fabulous 917 models to
qualify for the larger category. These exotic cars were
based on the 908/3, with a twelve-cylinder version of the
eight-cylinder engine. It was of 4.5 liters capacity at first

*Below: A classic shot of the latest Porsche,
the American-specification 962 endurance
racer.*

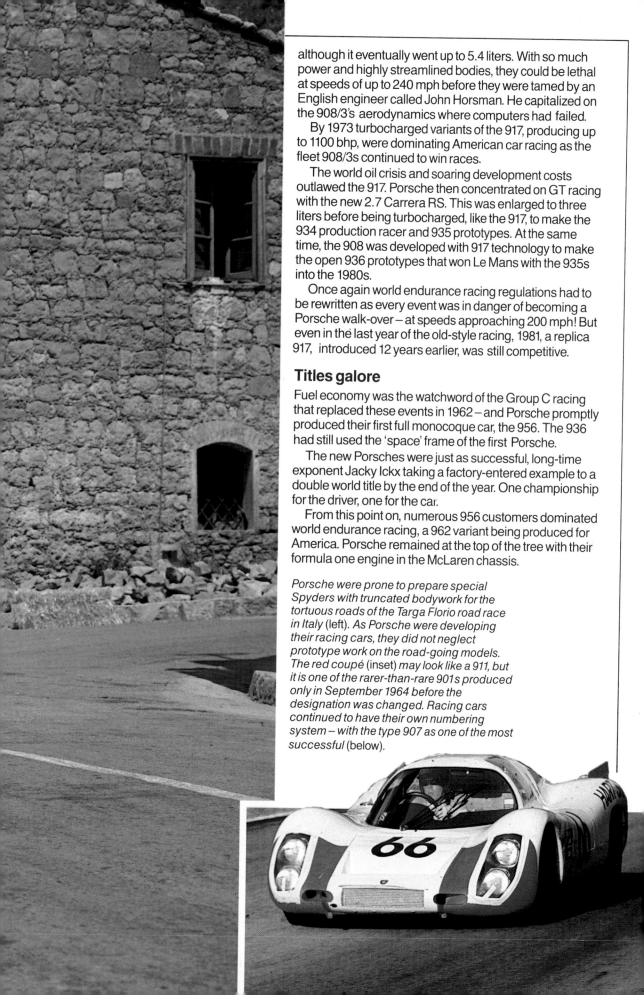

although it eventually went up to 5.4 liters. With so much power and highly streamlined bodies, they could be lethal at speeds of up to 240 mph before they were tamed by an English engineer called John Horsman. He capitalized on the 908/3's aerodynamics where computers had failed.

By 1973 turbocharged variants of the 917, producing up to 1100 bhp, were dominating American car racing as the fleet 908/3s continued to win races.

The world oil crisis and soaring development costs outlawed the 917. Porsche then concentrated on GT racing with the new 2.7 Carrera RS. This was enlarged to three liters before being turbocharged, like the 917, to make the 934 production racer and 935 prototypes. At the same time, the 908 was developed with 917 technology to make the open 936 prototypes that won Le Mans with the 935s into the 1980s.

Once again world endurance racing regulations had to be rewritten as every event was in danger of becoming a Porsche walk-over – at speeds approaching 200 mph! But even in the last year of the old-style racing, 1981, a replica 917, introduced 12 years earlier, was still competitive.

Titles galore

Fuel economy was the watchword of the Group C racing that replaced these events in 1962 – and Porsche promptly produced their first full monocoque car, the 956. The 936 had still used the 'space' frame of the first Porsche.

The new Porsches were just as successful, long-time exponent Jacky Ickx taking a factory-entered example to a double world title by the end of the year. One championship for the driver, one for the car.

From this point on, numerous 956 customers dominated world endurance racing, a 962 variant being produced for America. Porsche remained at the top of the tree with their formula one engine in the McLaren chassis.

Porsche were prone to prepare special Spyders with truncated bodywork for the tortuous roads of the Targa Florio road race in Italy (left). As Porsche were developing their racing cars, they did not neglect prototype work on the road-going models. The red coupé (inset) may look like a 911, but it is one of the rarer-than-rare 901s produced only in September 1964 before the designation was changed. Racing cars continued to have their own numbering system – with the type 907 as one of the most successful (below).

The 917 was only made really manageable when the British engineer, John Horsman, was helping run the blue-and-white Gulf-liveried cars (inset). He cut off the tail to improve high-speed handling, with the Porsche factory adopting the same style – sometimes with fins (left) – as the Gulf cars' lap times tumbled.

The early lightweight 911R racing Porsche *(below) was built with right-hand drive for more accurate placing on circuits which are predominantly right-handed. By 1978, the Porsche 911 had reached its most extreme shape in the long-nosed and long-tailed 935 (right), the body panels of which were simply tacked on to a standard shell!* Meanwhile Jochen Mass, Australian Vern Schuppan, and American Hurley Haywood, were to race the last of the space-frame spyders, the *936* (far right), at Le Mans in 1981.

By 1984, Porsche were back in formula one racing with Niki Lauda winning the British grand prix at Brands Hatch in his McLaren *(below)*, after Jacky Ickx had taken the marque to a double world title on the same track – but in pouring rain – with the 956 in 1982 *(bottom)*. Later developments of the 956, such as the 962 pictured during a dramatic pit stop at Le Mans in 1984 *(right)*, continued to dominate the great sports car races.

Some Porsches had a very long life in competition, the 908 pictured in 1983 having been built 12 years earlier! And the glorious old 2.7 Carrera RS from 1972 was still highly competitive in events as rough as the East African Safari rally in 1978 (inset).

PORSCHES FOR THE PEOPLE

No sooner had the Type 356 ended production and the 911 been established than it was apparent that Porsche needed a cheaper sports car to protect their sales from erosion at that end of the market. Initially they hoped that this need would be fulfilled by the Type 912, a 911 with the lower-priced four-cylinder 356 power unit.

It was soon apparent that the 912 could only be a stopgap because it cost almost as much to make as th[e] 911, and Porsche did not have the facilities then to prod[uce] enough really cheap cars to show a good return on the money invested. So they did a deal with Volkswagen. [The] old friends were to produce a sports car that could do[uble] up as a Porsche with a high-powered engine, or as a Volkswagen with cheaper running gear. It would be

engined because that seemed to be the way to go at
time; virtually every racing car had this layout by the
1960s.

omplete change

914 that resulted was not a great success, partly
use of a changing political situation at Volkswagen
h meant that the bodies cost Porsche too much to
e their version significantly cheaper than the 911, and
y because of uninspired styling, influenced by
rican safety dictates. It was also a question of image.
swagen, as it turned out, did not have a sporting
al in Europe, and Porsche, to the Americans, meant
re-bred grand touring car.
lkswagen saw the 914's boxlike appearance as the
problem and commissioned Porsche to design a new
p sports car for them. This would be a far prettier

coupé, using a large number of basic Volkswagen
mechanical parts to keep down the price. Volkswagen did
not mind Porsche working on a far more luxurious car at
the same time; the benefits would be mutual if their
appearance was similar. Volkswagen owners would want
to gear up to the new expensive Porsche, and Porsche
could spread out some of the development costs over
both cars.

But once again the political situation changed at

The neat and cleanly-formed 924,
introduced in 1975, was to become the first
really successful economy-priced Porsche
since the early 356.

Volkswagen, and the design for the new cheap sports car was dropped, only for Porsche to decide to produce it themselves. They had opted for water-cooled engines because their existing air-cooled units were noisy with no coolant to absorb the sound, and this was expected to become a problem with German legislation in particular. It was also felt necessary to concentrate a large mass of metal at the front of the car to meet ever more stringent American crash laws. So the new machines were front-engined as well as water-cooled, quite unlike the traditional Porsches. But they retained rear-wheel drive in the interests of the best handling and steering.

The most pressing need was for the cheaper car, a coupé because the Americans were expected to outlaw open cars on the grounds of safety. This was introduce[d] 1975 as the 924 and soon superseded the 914.

Once the 924 was well under way, Porsche felt that th[ey] could concentrate on the new super-luxury machine, th[e] 928, even though the 911 was still selling well – but sure[ly] could not go on forever? The 928 was given a large (4.[4] liter) V8 engine for the smoothest and most silent abilit[y to] meet what were expected to be severe emission regulations. It even got automatic transmission as part [of] its boulevard appeal – a feature that has never been popular on the 911. One of the strokes of genius that distinguished the 928 was the way in which bumpers w[ere] concealed behind flexible panels, in a far neater mann[er] than the 'tacked-on' beams adopted by competitors.

much choice...

928 was a superb vehicle and still is, but quite unlike more highly tuned 911. As a result it has tended to eal to customers who might have preferred a big oon, rather than to the sports car fans, who continued to or the traditional machinery.

orsche did everything they could to promote the 924 928, but 911 sales remained firm. Development was centrated on the front-engined cars, with the sportier S and the 924 Turbo, which had 928-style performance vo-thirds its price and half that of a 930. Then came the Carrera in 1979, hoping to take over the mantle of the 2.7 Carrera RS. Both new cars sold well, but they dn't kill the 911, and subsequently the 924 Carrera was

made smoother to drive with a power unit that was virtually half that of the 928. The resultant 944 appealed especially to the American market. Porsche enthusiasts had the best of every world with so many models from which to choose.

Although technically good, the box-shaped 914 – pictured here in Volkswagen guise (below right) – was too stark and expensive to be a great success. The 924's cheeky appeal was emphasized, however, when its headlights were raised (bottom left) and it became a popular wheel-wagging attraction at race tracks when a series of events was organized to promote the model in 1978 (top left).

The raised-and-lowered headlight theme (top left) *was carried over to the Porsche 928, which featured a rear spoiler on the S version* (top center), *exceptionally neat flexible plastic panels concealing sturdy alloy beam bumpers* (top right) *to help present a clean and uncluttered profile* (below).

The latest road-going Porsche, the 944 (above), is effectively a combination of the best aspects of the 924 (left) and the 928, featuring the 924's low-cost bodyshell and economy equipment and the flexibility of the 928 engine wih its four-cylinder unit.

The 928S remains at the top of the line in the front-engined class and one of the most desirable grand touring cars in the world.

Front endpaper: *Classic of classics . . . the Porsche 911 2.7 Carrera.*

Back endpaper: *One of the greatest endurance racers: the Porsche 956.*

Picture Credits

Neill Bruce Photographic 7 top, 10-11, 11 bottom, 12-13, 14-15, 17 right, 28-29, 32-33, 34-35, 35 top, 35 bottom, 43 top, 58-59, 60-61 top, 60-61 bottom, 61 top **Dianna Burnett** 8-9 **Daily Telegraph Colour Library** 60 top **Mirco Decet** half-title page, title page, contents page **Geoffrey Goddard** 18-19, 24-25, 25, 46-47, 47, 48-49 **Chris Harvey** front cover, front endpaper, 7 bottom, 11 top, 24 bottom, 27 bottom, 30-31, 31, 36-37, 39 top, 42-43, 43 bottom, 44-45, 46, 49, 50-51 top, 52 top, 52 bottom, 52-53, 54-55, 55, 58 top, 62-63, back endpaper **L.A.T.** 6-7 **Andrew Morland** 12, 20-21, 38 top, 38-39, 56-57 **Porsche Cars G.B. Ltd** 63, 64 **Peter Roberts** 26 **Nigel Snowdon** 22-23, 51 top **Tony Stone Worldwide** 27 top, 40-41 **Nicky Wright** 16-17, 17 left **Zagari** 18, 24 top, 50-51 bottom **ZEFA** 41, 58 bottom